PRAISE FOR *COMPOSITIO*

In *Composition*, Junious 'Jay' Ward resurrects personal, familial, and collective histories in striking and vivid language, each poem cinematic—a homecoming concert, a government document, a father tending a fire—and utterly unflinching. Ward's poems reach across every "in between", every denial, every burning, to seek refuge, finally, in the real story, the whole story. And we, the readers, are lucky to "fly / & dance & light" in their brilliance. This collection soars like a beacon, a bird-bodied music, sings "a whole bloodline toward a lesser wound".

— Jody Chan, *Sick*

Composition by Junious 'Jay' Ward takes the reader on a scenic poetic journey. This collection highlights the various ways a poem can be written by exploring forms and using line breaks as a tool that also tells a story. The approach that Ward takes creates an engaging experience for the audience while tackling issues such as race, colorism, and grief. *Composition* is a breath of fresh air and a necessary addition to any poetry lover's bookshelf.

— Rudy Francisco, *I'll Fly Away*

Erasures, contrapuntal, ekphrases, epithalamia—Junious 'Jay' Ward's *Composition* is like a formalist's fever dream. In his explorations of race, masculinity, language, and loss, Ward shows us how the self is formed and re-formed through the stories we tell and the documents we carry through life. *Composition* looks at identity the way a flipbook looks at an image.

— Michael Mlekoday, *All Earthly Bodies*

COMPOSITION

COMPOSITION

poems by

Junious Ward

Button Publishing Inc.
Minneapolis
2023

COMPOSITION
POETRY
AUTHOR: JUNIOUS WARD
COVER DESIGN: AMY LAW
GRAPHIC DESIGN: SHANE MANIER

ALL RIGHTS RESERVED

Published by Button Poetry
Minneapolis, MN 55418 | http://www.buttonpoetry.com

Manufactured in the United States of America
PRINT ISBN: 978-1-63834-047-8
EBOOK ISBN: 978-1-63834-053-9
AUDIOBOOK ISBN: 978-1-63834-054-6

First printing

Dedicated with love to my father, William Ward
(aka Joe, Joe Boy, Bill, Farmhand, Wardey, WeeDee, Willie, Dick, and collectively
when with his four brothers, Dem Ward Boys). 1939–1996

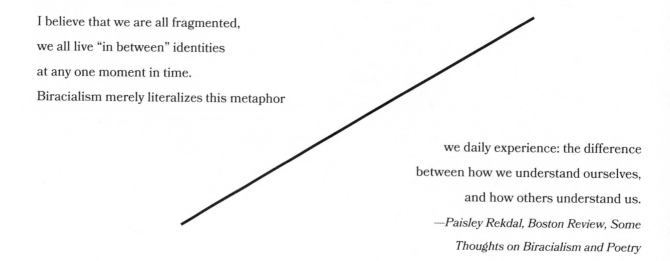

I believe that we are all fragmented,
we all live "in between" identities
at any one moment in time.
Biracialism merely literalizes this metaphor

we daily experience: the difference
between how we understand ourselves,
and how others understand us.
—Paisley Rekdal, Boston Review, Some
Thoughts on Biracialism and Poetry

Contents

I.

Kodak 4200 Slide Projector Asks if I Ever Held Hands with My Father   *1*

Epithalamium from Dad to Mom   *3*

#219   *4*

Let the Plantation Bear Witness   *12*

Spiritual Rising from a Cotton Field Burning   *13*

Homecoming, Rich Square, NC   *14*

Like Prophets of Baal   *17*

Within the Prohibited Degree   *20*

The Boy Is   *21*

Language of Composition   *22*

Do You Identify as African American?   *24*

Virginia Health Bulletin, Extra No. 2   *27*

Black Rapture   *28*

Ode to Black-*ish*   *49*

Concerning a Problem   *51*

We Learn in Halves   *54*

II.

Identity Gap   *64*

Mural of This Country   *66*

Etymology of 'Boy'   *68*

Jerry Jones Addresses His [Players] Regarding the NFL Boycott   *69*

The Makers   *70*

forever, a protest is just a run   *72*

Well-Intentioned Questioning of Black Joy   *74*

Everything Could Be a Prayer   *75*

Google Image Search: Boston Massacre   *77*

I Can't Stare Directly into the Footage   *79*

The Field White for Harvest but the Neighbors Saw Nothing   *80*

Southern Cross, Thirty Feet High   *81*

The Narrative   *82*

Tanka from Mom to Dad   *83*

Perception   *84*

Blessings   *88*

Mushroom Cloud   *89*

Imagine Me   *90*

The Speaker of the Poem Is Asked in Workshop about an Unsayable Thing and How It Relates to His Father but It's Too Loud to Hear Anything over the DeeJay   *93*

I Love the Hometown I Had to Leave   *95*

Inheritance   *97*

Notes

Appendix:

A: Bill of Rights for People of Mixed Heritage   *102*

B: Virginia Health Bulletin   *104*

C: SB 219, The Racial Integrity Act   *105*

D: NC Prohibits Any Marriage Between Races   *107*

E: Mildred Loving's Letter   *108*

F: Terms Formerly Used to Represent Degrees of Blackness   *109*

Acknowledgements   *111*

About the Author   *113*

COMPOSITION

I.

KODAK 4200 SLIDE PROJECTOR ASKS IF I EVER HELD HANDS WITH MY FATHER

I.

In the first picture
my father's hands

ain't holding nothing
but a cooking spoon

                I hold

the wired remote, clicking
to the next slide   a lifetime
                flashing against yellowed plaster

*

In this one his hands are   empty
near a hollow steel pot
first day as a cook at
Hudson River
State Hospital   where

he and Mom met   I imagine
there is a photo   his hand
focused on her belly
my hand walled within

                reaching impossibly
                toward

*

Here a custodian   his hands
covered in grease
& callus—hot water
heater memento He   really could
                fix/love
                whatever

needed to be
loved/fixed   if I'd let him

1

instead I'd pretend
not to see him in school
head down timid
waving as he passed

II.

Memory merges

light & dust
an odd hum

with the present—
hospital room

a blink of
machines oscillating

tethered

like

past lives against
a transfigured wall

his thin fingers
resting in mine

EPITHALAMIUM FROM DAD TO MOM

after my parents' wedding photo

Skip to the end—you have to know I'd still die
for it, to hold it all. You: Caregiver, Master of Loss,
Weary Hands. The boys: shades of us. Of course I
would risk the law, Town Hall, even the courthouse.

In fact, break open these doors—I'd meet you anywhere.
You: A-line dress, angled angel, halo of white headband,
look at me and say *promise*. I whisper into your nape:
we both shall live. Just outside our blessing

is called blasphemy, forbidden, hanging, strange,
a tree that was, and is not, and yet will be. In your belly,
a branch—fruit, wing—yes—a way. Steal away
south. *part*. Reunite like doves midheaven. We'll fly

and dance and light, sunlit as any new beginning.
have & hold. We don't have much but everything.

#219

A series of erasures of the Racial Integrity Act of 1924, Senate Bill 219

I. Self-Obsessed

Virginia   shall   be
        entitled   to   disbelieve

**(1. all laws heretofore, 2. intermarriage of white and colored persons,
3. vital statistics, 4. all acts inconsistent with this act, [or])**

the extent   repealed

II. THE LONG GAME

Be it enacted, any negro, or mixture thereof, personally registering
    shall be punished by the penitentiary.

For each registration properly made, the registrant
    shall be humbled by the penitentiary.

Marriage shall be granted to applicants of **pure** white race
    only, no **epithalamia sung in the** penitentiary,

save a white person. No other non-Caucasic blood
    shall avoid running from the penitentiary.

The **State shall** be paid, for the purposes of this Act,
    funded by the penitentiary.

All inconsistent with this Act
    shall **swell like light,** flooding the penitentiary.

III. LOCO PARENTIS

...tion of any individual, as Caucasian, negro, Mongolian, American Indian, Asian... any mixture there The state other non-Caucasic desires and if there be any mi... racial composition of the children it be ancestors, in so far as ascertainable. ...what generation such mixture occurred, may be certified by such individual, wh... known as a registration certificate. felony Registrar may supply to each local... number of such forms for punished of this and returned registrar may po... ly, as soon as possible after receiving said forms, have made thereon in dupli... of the racial composition as aforesaid, of each person resident in his district, ... before June fourteenth, nineteen hundred and twelve, which certificate sha... the signature of said person, or in the case of children under fourteen years of... signature of a parent, guardian, or other person standing in loco parentis. One of... for each person thus registered postage district shall be forwarded to the Sta...

IV. THE CYCLE

An Act to Preserve

Statistics

prepare

non-Caucasic strains, and

parents and   ancestors,   to show

every district

a felony.

wilfully knowingly making a false birth punished

properly returned to the State

The deputy shall use the same care

to save a white person, or a person with no other admixture of blood than white

white persons. heretofore and now in effect prohibited

necessary assistance

V. LETTER OF PROMISE

1. Choose one: All, Pertinent, No
2. Name of a government agency
3. Synonym for "outsiders"
4. Choose one: walking free, being one of us, it's too late
5. Race or ethnicity in America other than white
6. Third Person Pronoun
7. Choose one: immediately, eventually, de facto
8. Choose one: good, reformed, legal
9. Choose one: agents, cronies, mob justice
10. Choose one: monitor, unharm, profile
11. Choose one: melanin, "the talk" with a child, 400 years of systemic oppression prohibiting generational wealth
12. Choose one: poor, struggling, many
13. Choose one: incarceration rates, interest rates, blood pressure
14. A relative's job title
15. Choose one: neutralizes, divides, exploits

_____ personal information should be important to _____. For example, this is the law:
1   2

_____ must provide age and must register before _____. When a _____ child is
3   4   5

born, _____ will be sentenced to prison _____. Upon completion, to make sure the
6   7

candidate is a _____ citizen, testing is required. The police and their _____ must be
8   9

careful to _____ candidates. _____ are not allowed. In this country "white" means
10   3

means people who do not have _____. In the United States, _____ _____ people
11   12   5

report higher _____ than white _____s. This law prohibits marriage. To achieve the
13   14

goals of this law, it is important that the government _____ this group. This evil deed must
15

be forgiven.

LET THE PLANTATION BEAR WITNESS

did·n't bern—we ser·viv—you preech: we sin
you teech: hat skin—giv us: pork gut—we mak:
chit·lin cir·kit—allee nois—dark musik
we mak: blak lov—blak strong—strong lov—long day
lik Har·ri·ett: long day—Ebb Cade: long day
Hen·ri·et·ta: con·sent—den·id ag·in
we de·mand: cen·tral park—fiv stars—blak fivs
blak star—blak on—both sids—blak hous—blak livs

tell us: *go bak—stranj frut—bild wall—grat a·gin*
we mad: strong baks—hi yeeld—thorn crown—cuntry grat
cof·fers fild—pre·shus feeld—pal·pat·ing con·sent
de·nid ag·in—ag·in ag·in—de·spit kind·
ling harts—run·ning flam—jus ima·jin—the smok
tell mas·sa—*cott·in bern—be·fo us—blak fok*

SPIRITUAL RISING FROM A COTTON FIELD BURNING

When I call to you, love, call me Black
       as soot on an east wind.
Sway to my Black song, my proud dark,
       yes, my strut like brimstone.

Come to me as soot on homeward wind,
       nose to raincloud of rubble—say
folk smell brimstone where my thighs dance.
       Don't think me lifeless dirt, some folk'd say

simply a raincloud of rubble. No. Swear
       I'm eager to burst, to free, like pinions,
embers like seed. Some say lifeless, say dirt,
       but I lit it, *(O' lawd),* me. See how I become

sign in heaven. Swear, I'm eager to burst.
       Burning like a throat, burning like a sore.
Me. *(O' lawd)* I lit the tiny light that turns
       this wild land razed o'er & o'er

like a burning throat. Yes, watch me soar.
       Swaying to smoky song, dark and proud of
razing this wild, wild land o'er & o'er
       like a beacon, a calling, a Black love.

HOMECOMING, RICH SQUARE, NC

I.
Northern Black folk
drive through my hometown &
stop along the road
to pick cotton—a drifted piece,
something the machine skipped

over. Feel the need to connect,
honor ancestors by picking straight
from the claw of the plant's mouth,
seed and all,

how thorny it feels, how it calls
out blood like the Big Dipper sang
a whole bloodline toward a lesser wound.
How can anyone do this all day?

I worked that field as a kid.
Only once. Burlap skin
like thirsty hands during an annual
event (reminder) for families
in need of extra income.

Come, the Cotton Gin called.
Mighty fine job, sang Jackson Street
from its own crescent mouth.

How callused these hands
and strong this back, I dreamed;
tan this skin, eager this frame.
A man. A man. A bag

of white gold taller than my dusty afro
earned $8.58, a check that arrived
two weeks later. *Hell no,* I never went back.

II.

My mother-in-law had never seen
a cotton field up close, this visit

she threw open the door
before I even got to a good stop,

went elbow deep and picked
one tuft clean and good, nervous

the landowner might see her working
his soil and pick up a shotgun.

Noticed the blood on her fingers,
rubbed them pink,

and was quiet
the rest of the way home.

LIKE PROPHETS OF BAAL

We had gotten a whole hog
from Aulander, pink-fleshed
and splayed like a sacrifice
to cover sin, which is belief
that tomorrow is a place
we can eat.

I walk around the offering
before the body is pulled.

The men maneuver flame
and smoke seems to follow me
no matter where I go. Dad is gone

to tend the fire.

My uncle motions the bag toward me,
peels it from the bottle's mouth like
a fast-moving rain cloud. It burns sweet

on my finger. I look around nervous   [the way
          I would years later when the homeless man
          outside 7-Eleven returned with Mad Dog, OE,
          and something for himself].

That's good stuff, my uncle says, and I nod
in belief, face contorting into an amen.

But it burns. It burns

like the split-open swine on cinder-block.
See! How the smoke follows our gods
like eyes of a portrait, an heirloom.

The men walk in their own ritual
of pretense, ignoring whole conflagrations.

My uncle ignores hole burns in his chest.

Just like Dad.   [One day I'd beg Uncle Skin
          to put the cigarettes down.

          He'd say there's no point in quitting now
          when he could feel what was chasing him
          already had hold.]

Temple of blackened-breathing, charred
flesh, his lung is smoking in the pit,
it's right there, leapt from his torso.

We hop out his truck and the brown paper
cloud disappears under his seat, crackling
its own thunder.

He shows me how to coerce
embers back into flame while
he lights a Newport. Done:

the tradition handed down.

          [Decades pass and I still drink cognac,
          my throat an altar of wet ground, each sip
          proof, each taste a howl for resurrection.

          Bring it back, that moon, bring it back, his smile
          an introduction, a soft mischief.

          I don't even think Dad would've minded
          the Hennessy really, but I never told him.

          Most beliefs we build on secrets.

          When I say cancer runs
          in my family, what I mean is
          my father and his five siblings
          couldn't run fast enough.

What I mean is I ain't been back
to my hometown since this uncle's
funeral. What I mean is

Dad is gone. My uncle followed

like smoke. I'm being chased.

A monster's hot breath
searches for my lungs.]

I get down face-to-gnarled-face
with the animal whose skin pops.

I can smell the pork
ripen like impending rain
on the summer air.

I summon the fire now.
Swallow it. Like the men & gods before me

[I stretch a rod through billowing
  smoke to touch, to test, to measure
  a prophecy against an unforgiving sky].

WITHIN THE PROHIBITED DEGREE

The present Constitution of North Carolina says such marriages are "forever prohibited."

1963, six years before my parents' marriage

I grew up 52 miles from where this article was written

All southern states have such statutes

the children of a prohibited interracial marriage are illegitimate

Random memory: at the table I ask if I'm adopted, did they laugh?

The Supreme Court of North Carolina has said that a Negro is one who has one eighth Negro ancestry

I am measured and found wanting

it must be proved that this ancestor was of absolutely pure Negro blood. This might be extraordinarily difficult...   *absolutely pure*

it is a criminal offense in North Carolina for a person with the prohibited degree of Negro ancestry to marry a white person

Joe & Judy married in Poughkeepsie, NY. Moved to Rich Square, NC 1980

there were looks in church sometimes, momentaneous

the marriage is utterly null and void, and if they cohabit they may be indicted on a criminal charge of fornication

one would not be realistic...to conclude...the constitutionality of these anti-miscegination statutes will remain static in the light of the US Supreme Court's recently growing tendency to move forward whenever racial issues are involved

Loving v Virginia, 1967, three years before Tyrone was born

THE BOY IS

Public Enemy at full volume en route
to a New Hampshire summer is tongue-in-cheek
gospel like the yellow and green colorway
Nikes your dad got from the back of that truck.
Bootleg Huey P. in Lacoste on the school
tennis team. Kids said *fake* and you got angry,
not because they poked or questioned what was real
but because you didn't know and you should've.

You rush the net and life becomes a volley
of life lessons. You're five and Mom sits you down
to explain why kids made fun of you and why
you shouldn't be ashamed. You're fifteen and think
the only reason your biracial friends are
confused is because they never had that talk.
You're twenty and curb use of the word *sellout,*
opting for *we're all in this together, fam.*

Know there are limits, trying to prove yourself.
Hat backwards, baggy shorts and that certain swag
you picked up from years of practice. The cute girls,
just far enough away to think their whispers
are safe, debate themselves: *what you think he is?*
You lose the point in the tennis match and you
get angry, not because they distracted you
but because they didn't know and someone should.

LANGUAGE OF COMPOSITION

Zebra: what I was called in Kindergarten

Oreo: first grade, when told I talk like someone else's filling

Half-breed: somewhere in the years when 'boys will be boys' uncoiled from parents' lips natural as a garden snake

Mutt: by the raging boy with the patchwork dog

Mulatto: by my own voice, thinking it was a fancier form of self-deprecation, before knowing about the mule

Redbone: admittedly, I first learned this word after watching Boomerang where Halle Berry was the love interest and the object of desire was Robin Givens. The comic relief being the rejection of Grace Jones as a suitable bed partner, which is high-school-junior speak for 'love should've asked a light skinned girl to the prom last night.'

Racism: coined in New York, 1902, as a way to describe what must be destroyed, along with classism, by the same man who feverishly touted Borg-like assimilation via destruction of a mother tongue: kill the Indian in him...save the man

sacatra: a person who is 7/8 black. 87.5% black. a drop white

griffe: a person who is 3/4 black. also used to describe any person of mixed Negro and American Indian blood. 75% black. a dollop white, or equal parts other.

marabou: a person who is 5/8 black. 62.5% black. a scant white.

quadroon: a person who is 1/4 black. 75% white. a dollop black.

octoroon or metif: a person 1/8 black. 87.5% white. a drop black.

meamelouc or mamelouque: see sextaroon.

sextaroon: a person who is 1/16 black. 94% white. a dash black.

Linguistic Relativity: says our worldview is determined by the structure of the language we use—does it mean: simply framing the sentence gives it enduring truth, does it mean: I can only conceptualize a word through the eyes of its progenitor, does it mean: feeling regret over rubbish depends wholly on who threw it away

demi-meamelouc: a person 1/32 black. 97% white. a pinch black.

Americanish: the language of unsheathing in crowded spaces, of throw rock hide hand, of an ache I've sought approval from, of compulsion, of quantification, of other, of ether, of delusion, of revision, of the insatiable bite

sangmelee: a person who is 1/64 black. 98.5% white. a smidge black.

Bilingual: new medical form allowing choice of two races but still requiring one to be selected as primary, or a shopper feigning interest in a can of something they won't purchase while simultaneously pretending not to hear someone asking for help in a different language

mulatto: Based on the Spanish word mulo meaning mule, implying that the person is sterile like a mule, or implying "hybrid vigor," the idea that breeding across difference, as with dogs, creates a stronger, and more attractive breed. 50% black. equal parts white.

Americanish accent: to ignore what is not first understood, to smile "politely" as if choking on an inside joke, to speak on impulse like a fire parsing air for oxygen, to burn for the sake of the plume so that even an epithet's death is a head on a pike

DO YOU IDENTIFY AS AFRICAN AMERICAN?

This feels imposed or assumed,
a No. 2 pencil—a selection on exams
or medical forms or census

*

I'm not sure actually, tell me the rules again

*

Nah, I'm Black B. I ain't worried 'bout the test,
in fifth grade I'm sweatin' the pre-test, the red
bubbles probin' for (only) one answer
My aunt says *this country gon'*
treat you Black so you Black

*

I am what I
shade

*

A shaded circle—black, white, etc., or other
or other-other, or half shaded (three-fifths?)

*

Opposed to what?

*

Do you mean culturally or do you mean
a continent followed by a country followed
by a choice other people want me to make
to qualify how American I am?

*

How American am I?

                    *

Eavesdropping the punchline:
        fam, if you're African American, and she's Asian American
        and they're Latin American, what that make our white friend?
        American. Get it? A plain ol' patriot

                    *

It don't matter for real for real, when the ancestors
come callin' that *kum buba yali, kum buba tambe,*
        I'm out this piece

                    *

Yes, every time

9. **What is Person 1's r...**

○ White
○ Black, African A...
○ American Indi...
○ rincipal tribe...

IS A CONTINENT AND A COUNTRY

IS WHAT YOU MAKE. IT IS A SELECTION

IS A NUMBER TWO PENCIL DURING STATE EXAMS

THE WORLD GON' TREAT YOU BLACK

A CHOICE OTHER PEOPLE WANT YOU TO MAKE   A SHADE OF CIRCLE

IS A CONTINENT AND A COUNTRY

IS WHAT YOU MAKE. IT IS A SELECTION

A SHADE OF CIRCLE

IS BLACK BECAUSE MY AUNT SAID   IS BLACK BECAUSE MY AUNT SAID

THE WORLD GON' TREAT YOU BLACK

IS A NUMBER TWO PENCIL DURING STATE EXAMS

IS A COUNTRY THAT DOESN'T KNOW ITS OWN

A SHADE OF CIRCLE   A CHOICE OTHER PEOPLE WANT YOU TO MAKE

A SHADE OF CIRCLE

TO PROVE HOW AMERICAN YOU ARE.

IS BLACK BECAUSE MY AUNT SAID

IS A COUNTRY THAT DOESN'T KNOW ITS OWN

A SHADE OF CIRCLE

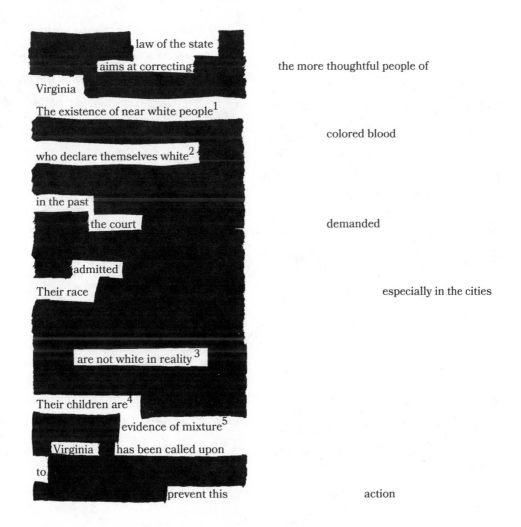

law of the state

aims at correcting   the more thoughtful people of

Virginia

The existence of near white people[1]

colored blood

who declare themselves white[2]

in the past

the court   demanded

admitted

Their race   especially in the cities

are not white in reality[3]

Their children are[4]

evidence of mixture[5]

Virginia   has been called upon

to

prevent this   action

---

1 10,000 to 20,000, possibly more, distinct colonies, holding themselves aloof from negroes.
2 And in not a few cases have intermarried with white people.
3 By the new definition of this law many will be observed who are scarcely distinguishable as colored.
4 Likely to revert to the distinctly negro type.
5 A slight extent it's true, but still enough to prevent them from being white.

BLACK RAPTURE

And they would walk up on the air like climbin' up on
a gate. And they flew like blackbirds over the fields.
Black, shiny wings flappin' against the blue up there—
The People Could Fly, Virginia Hamilton

Massa look'd up and seen   black bodies floatin'

right out the field, one   by one, a cloud of

freedom caught up   to glory like wings

on the seed of a   Black song. Travel

from massa's field   to my grandfather's

sharecrop shanty.   From there to

Selma, Montgomery, Greensboro.

From there the

seed

soars to

Sanford,

Ferguson, Baltimore. From there

out. Be all legs when Frankie

Be my Uncle Skin

a right big dinner.

tables at Conway Middle School.

Be Miranda

protest,

riot—

to fish fry by the lake, cook-

Beverly & Maze come on.

slumped in a chair after

Be me beatin'on lunch

cuffed, clipped. MawMaw   say, when that day come your

   wings gon' spread wider than   an archangel with a smile to

      match. I say, I can't   smile and open my back

      to the wind at the same time can I?

         She say, boy, don't you

            know you

            can fly,

change, become somethin' else   entirely? But y'all seen it.

    Reaction to change always   been violent, always been

        chase and hound and water hose. Reaction

            to change always been:

              Now

why ya wanna do that for?   *Why ya wanna go and mess*

    up a good thang? Why   *ya wanna not be satisfied*

      with what we gave ya?   *See, we never shoulda*

       gave y'all nothing!   *What are we gonna*

        do about Black Wall

          Street but

           burn it

38

down? What are we gonna do   *about Harlem but take it back?*

What we gon' do but tell ya   *what we gon' do and then do it*

and then ask ya why ya   *mad for, ain't ya grateful?*

Yes. We be grateful.   For Fannie Lou

Hamer, Rosa Parks, my Aunt

Clo, Aunt Hessie,

Mawmaw,

and all

the Black women who made   it possible for us to fly

in the first place. For   Solange & Viola &

Lupita & Tank   and the Bangas

& for me & you,   your mamma &

your cousin   too—grateful

for every lasting   song and too the

fleeting ones,   and too the

ones remindin' us we gon'

make it this time

like we

make it

every time. When they ask how   we did it, the answer ain't

love it's heart, not steadfast—   shift, not intention—

movement, not a wall—   Jericho. The answer to

any question is not   a trump that raises

a wall, it's a trumpet that brings

one down. What

work,

how

heart, why shift, when now,   where movement, who Joshua,

what ram horn, why fall,   why disrupt, who left the

gate open? If this the   plantation what they

gon' do without us?   —Look at this view—

how we get up so high

after being

brought

so low, ain't we beautiful? Oh   yeah, you got wings. Just

      'cause they forgotten or   called home or cuffed or

          clipped or planted down   in a distant deep like a

             rooted smile don't mean you ain't been

                 flyin' this whole

                   time.

ODE TO BLACK–*ISH*

I.
There's no logical reason why I've chosen
now as the right time to crush
on Tracee Ellis Ross. The earlier episode,
when she wore life into that romper
and everyone realized she had the shape
an onion would layer its tears for,
was a more appropriate time to swoon.

There's something about Bow and her eyes;
telling a story, relenting to the story,
listening as the story becomes a sitcom
flaunting its Blackness with banter, then bait-switching
to the industrial-strength-police-brutality version.
She first voices respectability politics, then turns
it all around, gets it. Genius. Beautiful.

II.
Not African American-ish, not I-need-
to-fit-in-to-your-definition-ish.
Not middle-class-and-turned-my-back-
ish. Black-ish. That super Black ish.
Like talkin'-reckless-in-the-barbershop ish,
or white-in-the-boardroom ish. Everyday
type ish. Clap-back-on-a-neighbor-

paranoid-loud-and-occasionally-wrong ish. Love-
all-people-but-especially-my-people ish.
Admitting-stereotypes-are-true-of-some-people-
that-don't-make-them-bad-or-weird-
white-people-do-that-ish-too ish.
Sometimes we laugh to keep from—good-
conversation-can-cure-just-about-anything ish.

III.
That episode though—pretense of humor falling
to the side like store-bought potato salad
at the cookout. Dre voiced every black
household's thoughts as Obama walked down an
incredulously wide and open street. Bow spoke
an apologist's tongue but found her way
in the end. I saw my kids

by seeing theirs. Remembered the intricate struggle
of explaining the world to the innocent.
My parents' generation didn't need to know
the whole story to know the story:
a re-run is a bad dream; nightmare /
verdict / non-indictment / vigil / hashtag / in every home
and yes / we watch this ish / syndicated.

CONCERNING A PROBLEM

blackout of the letter Mildred Loving wrote to the Attorney General

not black. I told the people so when they came to arrest me.

Dear sir:
I am[1]
we have ... a problem[2]

Violation of code 20-54 and 20-58

married

We

live

opposed to, in combat with, counter to, pushed upon, conflicted amid, dogfighting, versus

against

like the one we called home in Carolina, my brother born three years after this court case

a little

town

unthinkable

to leave
is

our home
to
enter

Home = skin, but there's only room for one

thrown into your skin?

jail

We
can't live   but   would

like to
families & friends

our

afford an attorney

I'm fascinated by intent— where is the line, how is it drawn, how often crossed?

cannot

Is this where it happened was it caesura, erasure, silence, emptiness— did the empathy of white space catch a tin eye?

represents acceptance (denial?) of blackness, like Peter of Jesus, which didn't make him less a disciple according to the Word

get in touch

the appeal —— Please help if
you're

the conditional

truly
Loving

action, surname, landmark civil rights case, embodies a mother's ferocity—a cub some distance off unaware

---

1 Residents of Central Point—Mildred's hometown—had an ingrained history of choosing to identify as anything other than Black.

2 Virginia's ruling class quickly lobbied to change the definition of "white" to include a person with 1/16 American Indian ancestry, known as the Pocahontas Exception.

WE LEARN IN HALVES

If the basket is defined by what it gathers,
we are beyond meaning, drawn **BOLD**

a square stance, hands balled into fists,
words balled into wind. The legs are trunks,
thighs a blaze. Everything is red except what is
black. Ancestors are a tree and a gate.

What is protection? What is Divine?
How does it smoke along either side of

being called nigger,

alchemy? Mother. Land. Gate. Tribe.
A terrain of wolves, lesson for goats.

When I speak of boldness, I speak, like Langston, of rivers,
of passageways that navigate and fill the body as precisely as
hookworm. I speak of every time I remember

What we gather is more than a sum. Always.
The soft mouth, also the fang. Red as blood-
thirsty fire. Old as divinity airborne amongst
ash, guiding home the restless and forgotten.
See now your star; tribe; gate ajar and jonesing;
divinity as feral as the day it was born.

We do not speak symmetric, where both sides
of an image must hold the same weight, that
is misdirection. We learn in halves; not the seas
but the elevated earth, the dark and rich soil,

even if it was someone else's memory, even if
the tongue sparked against flint or decayed
in a rotting mouth, even if the tree cried itself
to sleep and pulled its own roots like a sackcloth.

WHAT WE GATHER

BEAUTY UNFOLDS
FROM CENTER

BEAUTY UNFOLDS
FROM CENTER

Co-workers,
Hudson River State Hospital 1968,
see page 83

Wedding Day,
Poughkeepsie Town Hall, 1969,
see page 3

Richard and Mildred Loving,
1964,
see page 51

"the children of an interracial marriage
are illegitmate,"
see page 20

The erasure of Crispus Attucks,
see page 77

The spark of the American Revolution
see page 77

Martín de Porres, referred to as the patron
saint of mixed race people,
see page 75

"the purposed marriage is absolutely null and void.
Being a nullity, it is good for no legal purpose,"
see Appendix D

"sin is belief that tomorrow is a place we can eat,"
see page 17

"the men walk in their own ritual of pretense,"
see page 17

"gravel driveways announcing visitors,"
see page 95

"bumpy back roads in a blue pickup,"
see page 93

Ward's Black & White Grocery
see page 84

"this movement, this train,"
Conversation y Romare Beardem
see page 66

Illustration from The People Could Fly
by Virgina Hamilton
see page 28

Transposed memory,
see page 84

II.

IDENTITY GAP

after Kirwyn Sutherland after Glenn Ligon

Push →	I DO HAVE A RIGHT TO BEAR CODE SWITCH	← Pull	
Push →	A PALIMPSEST IMPRINTED OVER CONJOINED	← Pull	
Push →	TEXT A THIRD OR FIFTH OR DIMLY FAMILIAR	Pull →	
Push →	I DO HAVE A RIGHT BETWEEN ƎЯƎHTHERE	Pull →	
← Push	TO ACKNOWLEDGE PRIVILEGE LATCHING	← Pull	
← Push	THE SKIN LIKE VOLTAGE I DO HAVE A RIGHT	← Pull	
← Push	THE JARGON SLANG VERNACULAR LEXICON	← Pull	
← Push	LIKE CROWDED ROUNDS HERE I AM LORD	← Pull	
Push →	OF ANY VOCABULARY PERTAINING ESCAPE	Pull →	
Push →	GRANT OPPORTUNITY PARTY THE POSSIBLE	Pull →	
Push →	[it's undreamt fragments] THE NOW THE DON'T I DO	Pull →	
Push →	HAVE A RIGHT TO DIMINISH SELF FOR DREAD	← Pull	
Push →	OR I DO HAVE A BRANDED EAR OF CLAIM	Pull →	
Push →	I DO ACCEPT INTERIORITY I HAVE THE RIGHT	Pull →	
← Push	A MIDDLE PASSAGE MAYFLOWER	Pull →	
← Push	DARING ITS OWN NAME DUEL	Pull →	
← Push	AIM TRUE A STEADY HAND	Pull →	

I DO I WANT A MINE TO SOME KID ROD

A KIND MINE OUR MIND ORDERED

THEY A MIND OF MINE OR TIME MINER

I DO I MINE A MINE TO MINE

TO ADDENDED WORKER INSIDE

THE THEY THEY I DO I WORKER MINE A MINE

THE TODAY MINER WORKERSHIP MINORLY

THEY ORDERED MINER MINE I AM MINE

TO ANY WOODWARD WORKER OVER

CHART ORDERED THEY THEY ARE THEY

I DO I DONE NOW THEY THEY I DO

MINE A MINE OF MINE WHO MINE OVER

SO I DO I MINE A WORKER MINE OF

I DO A DONE THEY I ONLY MINE THEY THEY

A   MIDDEN   BARRAG   MAXIMOUS

DAMAGE   OIL   OVER   MAN DUKE

AIR   MINE   A   HUNTER   CHAR

MURAL OF THIS COUNTRY

collage of ekphrastics for Romare Bearden

Your train
photobombed its tracks across the mural of
this country, like stitches on a mortal wound.

Your color walked around and intimidated frames right off the wall.
Fair as it seemed, all eyes were on
moving dark bodies back and forth through time.

Each destination was a whistling reminder of
a suppressed collective voice,
tired feet, or a simple life with big hands.

Pittsburgh and Harlem called to you, beckoned
something over something else through an open window but
I believe you never left Charlotte except physically. Saw

Mecklenburg in every wooden shingle and every recurring theme,
the journey of Odysseus lauding
universally in the mother tongue of sight.

What train yard get us here, what rail we ride,
What shade is the smoke?
If creation is an amalgam of experience, who creates the creator?

We all do, we all sit and question
your brush, art springing from a birth we can see,
wide-eyed in the mastery of your scissors.

You, the ancient midwife. Should we hang on your stories,
gather brush to start this fire,
sit at the feet of your conjur woman making glue
from a melting pot? What did you do,

Romare? You made whole people,
borne from bond and paper and sharp things like
Southern recall—this movement, this train,
speaking all on its own.

Speaking all on
on its own, southern recall, this   movement,
this train, borne from bond and paper and sharp things   like Romare
—you made whole people from a melting pot. What did you   do, sit at the
feet of your conjur woman making glue, gather brush to   start this fire?
You the ancient midwife. Should we hang on your stories,   wide-   eyed in the
mastery of your scissors, your brush, your art springing from a birth we can see? We
all do, we all sit and question if creation is an amalgam of experience, who creates
the creator? What shade is the smoke? What train yard get us here, what rail we ride
universally in the mother tongue of sight? The journey of Odysseus lauding Meck-
lenburg in every wooden shingle and every recurring theme. I believe you never left
Charlotte except physically. Saw something over something else through an open
window but Pittsburgh and Harlem called to you, beckoned tired feet, or a simple
life with big hands, a suppressed collective voice. Each destination was
a whistling reminder of moving dark bodies back and forth through
time. Fair as it seemed, all eyes were on your color. Walked
around and intimidated frames right off the wall.
This country, like the stitches on a mortal
wound, photobombed   its tracks
across the   mural
of   your
                                 train.

ETYMOLOGY OF 'BOY'

Boy	a male child / if used offensively, a male servant of any age or inferior to or in subjection to or Black
Whipping Boy	scapegoat / he who would bear the sins of others on his own flesh / a savior? (see poster boy)
Good Ol' Boy	a respected man from the South / a man in a network of like-minded men, sometimes chose the whipping boy (if used offensively, see same definition)
Country Boy	knows and loves the country—as in he was raised a *country boy*—as in even when he moves away and makes friendships with the *boys* at work he will still defend the views of his country
That-A-Boy	(alt, attaboy)—as in an *attaboy* was issued from the good ol' boy to the country boy (see non-indictment)
Mama's Boy	one who clings tight to the protection of his mother [when she fails to protect him her pain will resonate through streetside memorials]—as in I always knew he'd end up a *mama's boy* (see poster boy) (see hashtag) (see name followed by ampersand, ampersand, ampersand, dash-dash-dash-dash, ellipses, etc.)
Poster Boy	example of don't do this and here's why (see warning shot or lack thereof)
Bad Boy	Black / good at being Black—as in that's a *bad boy* right there (see can't stop won't stop)
B-Boy	a dancer, the boy is forever a dancer—as in the air is all 808 and EQ tonight while the *b-boy* breaks (alt, BE boy)—as in conjugation of the I AM—as in the *b-boy* is forever—as in the b----boy is the most divine beat drop whose name cannot be said out loud

JERRY JONES ADDRESSES HIS [PLAYERS] REGARDING THE NFL BOYCOTT

(Partially redacted, may differ slightly from actual quote)

" . . . listen: a [   ] ain't no slave if you get paid
and a field ain't Antebellum if you on one

instead of in one. Don't confuse what we gave you
for something you earned. Wait. A cotton pickin' minute

ain't training camp hours just like good ol' pig skin
ain't chitlins, you conflatin' patriots with runaways.

Not my boys.   Hold outs might get cut. Where
is your hand—on your heart or wallet

or over your mouth? Yes, over your mouth—your
speech is free but muffled. Deep in the heart

of Texas we play for the lights and for the song.
Dance ███████. Dance ████████. I said: dance ███████!

I said: you know how many folk would kill to be you—
in this house, my house? I said: I love all God's

boys, but under these stars we just [   ]. Praise America
's team! You best show up, shut up and [   ]—that's just

how it is between owners and [   ]. You ~~people~~ entertainers
should know better, imagining your knee could change America

's channel . . ."

THE MAKERS

White folks hear the blues come out,
but they don't know how it got there. —Ma Rainey

I. Ma Rainey Speaks to Elvis

What a strange sound to mimic and call creation.

My rent been making a sound the same color as these keys.

I sang a song that broke my own heart more than once—

mind you, that's even when I didn't hit the right notes.

Can't take that. Hard as you try you can't.

Can't thank the grass for rain while a cloud is watching.

II. The Ghost of Elvis Apologizes. Kinda.

I've only died once / so I wouldn't
say I was good at it / or anything
but I did make a tune / didn't I
could sing a song so blue / and black
you would swear / I colored / the chords
I been thinking / about how thrifters
pop / tags and sell something inferior
to the original / for more than it's
worth / and I know my work was not
in vain / I know I'll live on / there will never
be another me / how could there be
my soul wasn't even mine.

III. The Music Speaks for Itself

The smoke
cleared, exposed
your dissipatin
wisdom. I been
waitin to burn
red-faced and neck
bent back, waitin
for the curtains—
storm clouds breakin

like records—
to be pulled back,
to shake n shimmy
n sweat, to grunt
n falsetto n coo,
to slide one leg
like a pastor
slick cross
the floor,
finger extended,
to say now that
there, son,
that's how
it's done

FOREVER, A PROTEST IS JUST A RUN

-on sentence written without hands or gods & never stems from the march-turned-waterfall of bodies pouring over a police car like wanton flame, notice—none of the news outlets refer to these folk as animals or thugs or degenerates & no one says the aftermath makes it hard to take their protest seriously 'cause really they were just expressing themselves after their football team lost or their soccer team won or a statue came down & who even wrote the sentence (if we are speaking legalities) when elsewhere a man walking backwards is a threat, Ralph Ellison's gun is a threat, every shroud that names us *Exaggeration* is the body cam footage finally released but only partial so Fox News quotes Rodney King instead of Martin Luther King: *can't we all just get along* & maybe they don't know what King actually said was *a riot is the language of the unheard,* 'cause they were too busy not hearing it while the boy died or the girl was kicked or they both died twice; buried by stacks of resistant limbs 'cause justice is irresistible—my question is if Trump says bad cops are human & make mistakes too & then a cop in the sky is quoted as saying the guy with his hands up looks like a bad dude & later a white supremacist is taken alive & to Burger King after killing everyone in the church—are we praying to heaven or feeding an idol, or maybe the question is how do we do this so it makes sense, stops when it's supposed to, why do we have to break rules in the name of clarity just to be scolded for use of particular grammar—notice my hand is not in this, the ink keeps moving on its own, red & indelible, notice how tiring it can be (not seeing color), we see blood & you see black, we see protest & you see black words, we see poetics & you see ceaseless volleys that pain the ears but go unheard, become an exodus labeled *Beast,* meaning it's easier to focus on words than injustice, broken windows than oppression, meaning if it exposes you as the problem & you yelp & I misquote King, *a hit dog will holler* or I misquote God *we will tire out if we don't win the race for life,* then & then & then & then I will stand on a street corner in my Sunday best screaming all the scarlet text at apathetic passersby: *who wrote this poem but you, who but the zealot who scribes himself holy*

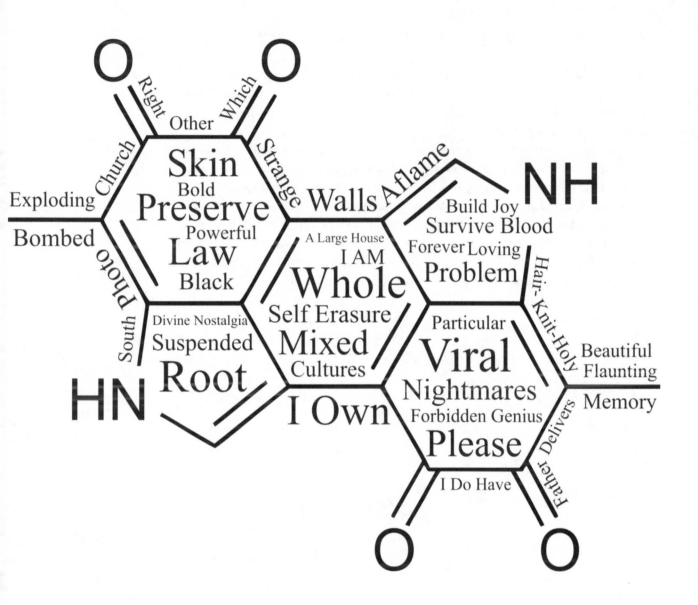

73

WELL-INTENTIONED QUESTIONING OF BLACK JOY

Why does joy have to be Black? Or so Black? Why not tan? What about a nice khaki-tinted joy alongside the many other joys in this world that don't alienate or exclude or escape my own perception of what joy is? Isn't that jubilance—me defining your joy by what renders me euphoric? Can't all our joys just get along, like, what if I bring my joy and yours on a play date to a place I know always turned my joy's eyes into filaments? This way I could expose your joy to real joy, civilize it, so to speak— we wouldn't have to call your joy Black anymore, yeah? We could just call it *all*— what a slogan: *ALL JOYS LAUGHTER*. What say we smile together in a "this'll prove to my co-worker calling the police was a one-time venture based on unfamiliar faces in a gentrified setting amid a really bad day for me (and you know that) plus what a good look for next year's Facebook memories" kind of way, which is to say smile so as to publicize the shade of our gums without implicating the sharpness of the teeth.

EVERYTHING COULD BE A PRAYER

Martín de Porres is recognized as the patron saint of mixed-race
people & public health workers & all who seek racial harmony.
Credited with many miracles, Martín died of fever in 1639.

I won't pray to you, Martín, but if I did how would that even work,
me to you, you for me, or jettison all hope
of intercession and just kick it dorm-room style? Pink and fevered
as a baby, my body may have passed
your bronze statue on the way home from Vassar Brothers Hospital.
Mulatto dog. Slave-son. Rebel of soft heart.
We've been called many names, but I'd never seek my own sale to save
a convent (unless you're thinking of convents as a way
we house faith, or the myriad of small faiths we call home—a name
versus what will truly follow a person).
The early whisper of morning's mouth in the green ragtop's
backseat hid mason jars for Tyrone and me
to pee in. After we moved to dad's hometown in Carolina
we'd visit New York each summer, stopping
at a trusted truckstop with a heat-lamp halo perched over day-shift
burgers. I wouldn't know this for decades
but as a teen my father had been taken by the Ku Klux Klan
or by the police or by some white men or all
of the above, and was miraculously released on the third day,
Grandpa Bud serving as mediator.
It makes me question whether surging out the South the way we did
whenever we traveled north, each precaution,
was ritual or prayer, a lasting standard by which a father delivers, watches
over. Are all such choices so clearly black
and white (I'm asking if salvation is without consequence)?
I feel obligated to say here, talking to you
like this does not constitute supplication. I speak to many selves,
especially in light traffic, who are dead or holy
or exist only as a voice in my thirteen-year-old Camry, a fervent recycle

of breath, disembodied but not ghost. To say I revere you—
as opposed to saying we cohabit our skin—is to say you prompted a white
dietician from Mass and a Black Army cook from Rich
Square to the same city of winding mazes, cleared a hand over them, said
in the blessing of this union I shall be reborn,
and kept them safe so that I'd be in position to move my own three children
across Mason-Dixon borders, across darkness,
to what we hoped was a better life. No, I can't believe in us. Father.
Risk taker. Saint to those whose eyes
are tinted with need. We are many names if we choose
not to believe in coincidence.
I'm not what you would call a believer of all miracles, but I give you this:
bilocation. You could appear beyond a locked door
to minister to the ill, they say, while also kneeling in the dankness
of your dormitory across the courtyard.
I assume these accounts owe much to the ebbing cognition of the sick, the time-
lapsed dispersion linked with intermittent
consciousness. Still. This might be the miracle I fall unto like revelatory light:
residing in two truths at once,
place & time being subjective, alone in a crib of night sweat,
a cool, damp towel pressed, somehow, to my face.

GOOGLE IMAGE SEARCH: BOSTON MASSACRE

Crispus Attucks speaks to Colin Kaepernick

We tiptoe the line
of protesting and provoking,
don't we? Suffer a kind
of death like a hero,
a martyr. Takes awhile

but searching our name
eventually shows a Black
man wounded, bleeding,
mulatto man with a song
overtaking the mouth.

How could we be disrespectful
to an owner? We were never
slaves. Call us uppity
even though we done worked
every job likely to kill us.

Say we run for a living
but it ain't that simple—men
looking to take our jobs, livelihood.
I don't know if I would go
as far as to say "patriot"

when the country I fight
for hides my skin but accepts
the revolution it sparks.
                    America!
renamed us nuisance

but history will concede
our place. I was there at the dawn
of it, hero, thug, unlikely
woolen-afro framing
my face like freedom

is framed, falling like my body
needs to be convinced it cannot
stand—there I am—fell
to a knee, sputtering like a song
is stuffed in my mouth.

I CAN'T STARE DIRECTLY INTO THE FOOTAGE

for Tamir Rice

What I saw was a tree waiting for the sun's return,
as the cycle dictates. Everything feels swept-back:

foliage varicose-veined and weighting the canopy, each fall
a vigil for the young, the perfect-bodied, individual leaf.

Invisibility is a weight. Like snow or like black-
shroud burden, child of a heavy branch bowing

to wind. No age or proper season, just weight. Invisibility
means leaves spill to the ground and no one considers the holes.

Cops chit-chat around the body they plucked, wait,
heave an entire shadow box to frame the story,

walk the weighted-with-color pavement. Yes, I saw
it all: the tree trunk—gray as the park's drawn-out thaw,

the cruiser's open maw—teeth bearing down on a weightless
leaf, the falling, the falling, the line of trees unable to turn away.

THE FIELD WHITE FOR HARVEST BUT THE NEIGHBORS SAW NOTHING

for Lennon Lacy

a swing set
becoming
hair-knit-holy
blossoming
puff-white
despite being
blown
heavenward

a suspended body
again dark root
never in place
Southern fruit
with seed
quivering stem
like a dandelion
spreading

a pendulum
creeping vine
jealous-stretched
hanging weed
a picked flower
a whisper
across a field
by careless children

SOUTHERN CROSS, THIRTY FEET HIGH

for Bree Newsome

waving in our faces, preening where it ought not,
puffed-up with pride and planted in so-called holy ground

as if we are not worthy to approach. *Snatch those ol' dixie stars, Bree,*
claw a clawing thing from a rent sky! Obama

said this bit of cloth belongs in a museum. You held history
in your hands like a living thing, choking. Those confederates

shrilled—*Rebel!* Yelled—*Vandal! Heritage*
not hate'd you like emancipation

wasn't a business decision, like slave states
didn't lose the war and throw blood into the sky

like a public hanging for a hundred-fifty years
the way a victor does. *Rewrite the kingdom,*

desecrate the flesh, swallow! These Galileans
gouge a mouth and don't expect the speech

to be shocking. *The museum is torn away!*
I imagine what you saw, raised up like a crystal stair:

something new, the congregation awestruck,
an easier God-sight without heritage

to block the view, your own image
coming on a cloud stretched to a flagging star.

THE NARRATIVE

The stories tell so similar I can't tell if I'm dreaming or
remembering hands pinned to ground, hands penned
writing some manacled vision of the future.

Hands behind the wheel or up, a toy gun, a licensed gun
—daughter watching, mother watching, father, son, cousin.
The stories be so similar I can't tell if I'm dreaming or

reaching for my ID, stepping out of the car, compliant, viral.
The assassination will be Live, my brother, viva la revolucíon,
igniting some Orwellian vision of the future.

No text by 10 p.m. No call by midnight. My biggest fear—
babygirl gets pulled over and I find out through social media.
The stories are so interchangeable I can't tell if I'm dreaming or

the body camera was turned off. I know you're tired of this poem,
its nagging anticipation, its blame-song, its gnawing complaint,
all poems, inviting some pissed-off vision of the future like—

open up, hands where we can see 'em, he's got a gun! he's got a gun!
But I assure you, I am shopworn writing this poem, more than you are
of hearing. These stories—so kindred, I can't tell if I'm dreaming or
fighting everything, everything in me, to envision a future.

TANKA FROM MOM TO DAD

after a photo of my parents at work smiling in white

my dove, I hear them:
      impossible   wrong or   *just*
look out the window

obtrusive as day-moon   bold
      as love
      our lives
a tracked flight

PERCEPTION

I mean you're [   ] but not like [   ] [   ].

A joke, a slur, a cosign, I don't know. Quantify? I lumber through time with words, I scissor a hole in my pocket, sandglass trickling down my leg.

A classmate feels comfortable repeating nigger/nigga in earshot? Something plausibly deniable like rapping a Snoop verse when the jam is being pumped up and all voices are meshed into a matted ball of knots. Or was there no music at all, an unraveling yarn, a retelling of someone else's words with detailed accuracy, the compliment of assimilation, the percussion of bloodrush vibrating every surface in the room? Ka-thump. Ka-thump.

Not [   ] people, [   ] people are cool, I'm assured during World Civ, *it's just those* [fill in ethnicity and corresponding stereotype here]. Hard to look at a [   ] friend the same after that, knowing the fill-in-the-blank depends on who's present.

My dad's playground proverb was: *if they talk bad about other people to you, you can best believe they talk bad about you to other people.*

*

Kindergartners lose stuff, simple as that. Hats, gloves, jackets, toys, anything not riveted, attached, or ingested. My mistake was putting that T-shirt in the trash thinking it wouldn't be seen.

Your mother is [   ] your dad is [   ], simple as that, my parents pointed out. Matlock, who'd be on tv that night, would be proud. *Let them talk, won't change nothing.*

I had run my mouth though. It's true what they say: kids who live in zebra shirt houses shouldn't throw mama jokes.

*

Thing is, most summers in New Hampshire with my grandparents was just me. At some point Tyrone's summers were filled with Little League, bat swinging like any number of poses from his favorite cards instead of picking June bugs off the rhubarb early in the morning, swimming in Silver Lake, or occasionally traveling to Conway for a pepper-bottomed slice of pizza in a building that looked like a barn. Or was it the baseball card shop that looked like a barn? Weird.

Is there a word for feeling safe yet conscious of your race(s) at the same time? Is that word dependent on your surroundings? Can I say something like "softknife" and it conjure a vision of me magnetized to my grammie's thigh while I catch the manager's eye tracking me from the door to the Reggie Jackson rookie?

*

Jay ain't gotta worry about that,
he probably never get stopped.

*

My best friend came down with so-called jungle fever in 8th grade. Didn't last long. A couple weeks maybe. Quick as a pack of firecrackers. Quick as the parents finding out.

Oh he don't like [   ] girls no more. She ain't that cute, just got blue eyes.

My dad and one of my four uncles married [   ] women. At the reunion I learn to read eyes like cards, cuttin' like the first book a spade takes, the hollerin' and risin' from the table, the signifyin' nature of the game.

*

In one memory, when I talk
about lugging the Fat Albert
lunchbox and a pillowcase
up the long asphalt driveway
of our Poughkeepsie home,
convinced I must belong
to another family, Tyrone
tells me it was actually him,
that I wasn't old enough to run
away at the time, let alone
remember. In a more recent
memory, he says *that was you*
not me. Which memory
was transposed? In which
did I become, for a day,
who I've always wanted to be,
pulling him along in my classic
Radio Flyer wagon, easy, one
hand behind my back?

*

During the months Dad and I were fighting about almost everything and I didn't want to be a Baptist anymore, we sat on the tailgate of his truck. He straightens up, tells me *listen: a man can only pass on two things to his son,*

(I'm expecting a variant of the "stay [   ] & die" idiom)

his name and his religion.

*

For a short while, my parents owned a convenience store just up the street from Creecy Elementary—Ward's Black & White. I know this sounds naïve but I heard "black & white" the way most folk would hear "five & dime." The name had a music to it and honestly, I'm sure I'd graduated high school before I realized how suitably on-brand it clanged at the corner in town, uvula of a cracking bell.

*

I joke that Tyrone's straight black hair,
which he's kept cut close for years now,
makes him look racially ambiguous, but
he is discernibly [   ], or at least for a
certainty not [   ]. We've never spoken
to each other about our individual
navigation of "[   ] spaces," certainly
not how I often felt less [   ] because I
appear to be less [   ]. Toward the end
of a speech he's giving, both sides
of our family present, he points
me out, talks about a polarized
nation, the instinctive nature of our code
switching, duality—all the mechanisms
we'd taught ourselves. I do understand
explaining a joke makes it less funny.

*

I am:

    a. the race(s) I choose to be or gravitate toward

    b. the race(s) others assume of me based on environmental factors

    c. the race(s) of the relative I most resemble

    d. neither and all of the above

In contemplating [dominant race]ness, my mind falls upon Schrödinger's cat. Complexity and nuance are predictions. I am technically both and neither of my races. The cat is dead. The cat is alive. This is theory.

I enter the room radioactive. I leave the room a [   ] cat. The room doesn't _____. The shadow bends over the walls, the _____ is a softknife.

BLESSINGS

my black family reunion is jealous   my white family reunion is jealous

they are covetous of each other's things

my mom's folks use two picnic tables   while the other reunion requires a resort

one is intimate and one is swollen

this one; we all here despite the odds   that one; more kin than you ever seen

attendance percentage v. actual numbers

but jealousy peeks through when   over a busy, packed-calendar summer

my kids can only tamp down a suitcase for one

they don't get to see parts of themselves   where are the jokes, the cousins

they missed growing up

driven by instinct, I react as mediator   playing dozens or spades at the picnic

praying over fish-fry hushpuppies

praying over burgers and dogs   what we remind ourselves of is this:

it is important to give thanks for

everything that seems a given   every member able to torque a schedule

the meal that brings us together and

fills our spirit like heaping plates, leads us   outweighs envy, no one eats until the prayer

confirms how one we are

MUSHROOM CLOUD

You think you love God so much, you think God made bad hair (laughs),
and made good hair? (laughs) and you still like Him? —Dick Gregory

Understand. It's not that I agreed with the rabbit hole I found myself
in, threading mortality with a strand of black hair, killing me, it's just
that I'm reminded of white classmates, quips bold as bullets, holding
their arm to mine, saying the sun loved them more than me, blacker.
Their blacker arm saying to mine the sun loved them more than me,
but my hair and its volume wasn't trying to hear all that—skin

& scalp & weapon & target, the mix. Mom gave me a bowl cut—
placed a salad bowl on my head and cut around its edges. No fade.
Haircuts! Bobby said *it's a violation of God,* said from the back
my head looked like an atom bomb, and all the black kids laughed.
All the Black kids looked and laughed like an atom bomb. My head
—God twisted it. It got to go through those coils. That's the God

talking to you. That night I attempted to disprove any mystery
locked in my follicles, clearing brush, bush. Mountains recede
in the wake of Mom's clippers. *Bullet proof vest—that's what nappy hair is.*
I felt less powerful (maybe it was vulnerability) like Samson—his wanting,
his vulnerability (maybe it was less wanting I felt). Like Samson, powerful
coils of afro on the floor like nuclear fallout induces an awakening;

their armed mouths claiming the Son loved them more and I
laugh like an atom bomb, laugh at the Blackness of it all,
the vulnerability, and feel powerful. All this God-strength
won't stop us being shot but it'll change the rhythm so we don't die.

IMAGINE ME

I. Playing the quadroons, middle school, at the wrong lunch table

where I ain't cocktail, I ain't chemistry class
beaker, I ain't Pit and Black Lab, I ain't sound
studio hip hop 'cross subwoofers and tweeters,
ain't a review of the latest Cole album—

don't call me mix-taped, confused, half
what you want, half what you tolerate.
Black history month ain't just 14 days
for me. There is no struggle for light

and dark within me. My skin has not revealed
a George Lucas plot-hole, I ain't a light version
of bad or a Sith variant of Jedi. I ain't a %
or a poor hand in spades, don't call me one

and a possible. I ain't forked tongue, duplicitous
speech, like you casting well-intentioned daggers
talmbout *"best of both worlds"* where my pigment
is the punch line concealed under your breath.

II. Filling in the circle, as required, before moving on

a yin and yang remix to Desiigner's song "Panda"
ending in two chords played at once, contrapuntal
on piano where all the keys gray into themselves,

my brother and I side-by-side while a stranger questions
the hammered strings under the lid and who makes
the better music while who might be more readily

applauded, or the light blue T-shirt I wore in kindergarten:
a dazzle of zebras frenzied across a vague plain, too tempting
for classmates, too wild with agency, too on the nose.

III. In a dystopian society born from your comments about babies

where the future is as beige as the children. All races
and cultures blend into a blinding chorus of kumbayas.

Every music video looks like Drake featuring Drake.
Even the Republicans say we are one people now,

and the liberals really don't see color anymore.
The pandas are gone.

Every face is a paper bag. There's only two
boxes on your medical form; other and not other.

There's a stigma about bringing non-mixed love interests
to meet your parents—*the horror, just think of the kids;*

confused throughout school. World history badgering:
what could've been, why so cruel, lighten up—

could privilege, even if it wanted, deny itself through laughter?
A joke can forecast unspeakable things and thirty years

later the teller regrets or denies. Saying "they always come
out so beautiful" means to dig a hole deep enough to bury

the prophecy you set in motion. Disavowing the prophecy
is to say *I don't think you understood what I meant.*

THE SPEAKER OF THE POEM IS ASKED IN WORKSHOP ABOUT AN UNSAYABLE THING AND HOW IT RELATES TO HIS FATHER BUT IT'S TOO LOUD TO HEAR ANYTHING OVER THE DEEJAY

another poem about your death where the sky opens you fall like a dove
another poem to eulogize you in a room you are absent from the concert

was amazing I got home after curfew just trying to escape the coma and
decision about life support the house dark my brother leapt off the living

room sleeper soon as I turn the key and I knew what that meant I always
rode shotgun through our one-traffic-light hometown adopting shortcuts

lost to me now roads tossed and tangled in hazy vignettes I can't loosen
the hospital's grip I've never one time forgiven myself one time driving

home from Elizabeth City's homecoming concert in late-early hours
blindsided by a swerve I woke up indebted to familiar pardoning roads

*

we tried the limits of awkward silence staring straight ahead on bumpy
back roads in that blue pickup where you'd occasionally ask about school
but most times repeated the black-father-catch-all phrase   *mmmhmm*

your way of filling the silence saying you heard or were skeptical or proud
of me or you _____ me sorry I've never said this out loud my therapist asks
so you learned doing something for yourself always ends badly would you
say that's been a recurring theme in your life   *mmmhmm*

the concert was amazing Nas Busta I freestyle battled some boys unloaded
on my best friend a thousand justifications to why I'm even here the doctor
says what started in your lungs marched to your throat a uniformed band
announcing its allegiance its victory its deep percussion and clash-clash-clash

through the body you slip away eyes closed and not conscious
I whisper I _____ you your fingers resurrect long enough to squeeze
my hand and I know I know it like the sound of a key turning dead-

bolt in workshop I tell teacher this was the same night you passed
not two days earlier that these same salt-rubbed hands were there
to hold Mom and I bury my face in everything my cohort believes
about me I've never forgiven the room myself the reason I was absent
I fall into my brother's shoulder and mutter something like *deserve* why
sorry I've never said this out loud I wasn't there when you _____

*

what face does forgiveness wear
      I need to say to someone *I love you*

the sky opens I need to say to someone
      I forgive you and look he's right here

can you   _____ me can you
_____ me   can I   _____ me can you
say it   can I   _____ me and mean it this time
               mmmhmm

I want (dad) to come home   but the roads are
dreamlike or from   a falling dove or
a tongue anointed   shotgun

I don't remember every detail
the score   walking from the field
to the quad lighthearted despite the loss

the afterparty going black
      then rattling
I was coming back I was
      lost to a sea of hands dimming
lights turntables scratching
themselves alive

I LOVE THE HOMETOWN I HAD TO LEAVE

Rich Square is a small town with a pull
strong as nostalgia. Small
like an atom you need to stay and escape
from, split without exploding.

I grew up in the chemtrails of segregation.
My white mom went to the Black church,
not far from the white church.

My white friends took a different bus,
played at the same school but never
the same house, grew up under the same flag.

I played in the woods, or on Creecy Lane
with the two Maurices, pig farm across
the street, cotton field down the road,
corn next door, humid, hot, and hazy.

Gravel driveways announcing visitors
like a crunchy doorbell. One stop light.
Pickup trucks and white friends—
both with Confederate flags.

Water hoses doubling as water parks.
Cadillacs and tractors. Dirt roads and street lights.
Juxtaposition is common, like South moving North,
like New York cousins boomeranging back
to this ground. Home is a return to dust, root.

Of course I remember Black kids being told
the pool in Jackson was closed while dozens
of kids could be seen splashing over a shoulder.

Of course I remember being followed
in the store for a zebra cake, called "boy,"
him tapping his waist. But what brings me home

is what's inevitably mine; riding around
Chapel Hill Road like I own this, the bridge,
the graveyard my father is buried in, home
of the Rams like I own this, return of the bubble

goose, cornbread and corner-store swag, like I own
this, Mad Dog like I own this, Southern Comfort,
Boone's Farm, Strawberry Hill after the football game,

Spirit Week bonfire with kids who make temporary
friends with buying-age bums—symbiosis of sorts,
Styrofoam cups, 8 Ball—an Olde English accent

sloshing to asphalt for the homies like I own this,
recurring orbit like they know my name still.

INHERITANCE

I was never the clean plate, I was the swirl
of flour-white biscuit in dark corn syrup.
At church I was a wide-mouthed Baptist hymn
whenever my father made eye contact.

Eight teabags bathing in a glass jar on the back steps,
sun high and fevered, I was a hot summer.
Who cares what the package says,
I was two cups of sugar instead of one.

I was Man-Man or Baby or Dee,
I was cousin Peanut from down the street.
A name in the South is a yardstick.
To measure legacy against a house is to say

Anthony shouldn't have taken the name Ten Pointer
after scoring ten points in a game. You think my friend
didn't love his family? What's that say about Uncle Alpo? Crack?
The senior in college who only let us call him Mynigga?

I remember, during an argument, Dad insisting
the only way he can pass on his name, as reflection, and
his religion, as heirloom, is a son—what is he if I'm
walking away from either? But I wasn't the clean plate.

All my life I only called myself Black, not
white. Black. Which
felt like the only way to keep part of him with me,
to acknowledge what I'd been given.

*

To acknowledge what I'd been given
felt like the only way to keep part of him with me.
White. Black. Which?
All my life I only called myself Black, not

walking away from either, but I wasn't the clean plate.
His religion, as heirloom, is a son—what is he if I'm
the only way he can pass on his name as reflection? And
I remember, during an argument, Dad insisting

the senior in college who only let us call him Mynigga,
didn't love his family. What's that say about Uncle Alpo? Crack?
After scoring ten points in a game, you think my friend
Anthony shouldn't have taken the name Ten Pointer?

To measure legacy against a house is to say
a name in the South is a yardstick.
I was cousin Peanut from down the street.
I was Man-Man or Baby or Dee.

I was two cups of sugar instead of one,
who cares what the package says.
Sun high and fevered, I was a hot summer,
eight teabags bathing in a glass jar on the back steps

whenever my father made eye contact
at church. I was a wide-mouthed Baptist hymn
of flour-white biscuit in dark corn syrup.
I was never the clean plate, I was the swirl.

NOTES

#219: Source text is the Racial Integrity Act of 1924 (SB 219). See Appendix C. Part V: Letter of Promise utilizes output from an app called Bad Translator which was used to translate the original text of SB 219 into a random foreign language and then back to English in a process that repeated 40x.

Within the Prohibited Degree: Source text is 1963 Rocky Mount Telegram. See Appendix D.

Language of Composition: Terms and definitions found on the right margin are excerpted from anti-miscegenation laws by state found on the Tennessee government website. See Appendix F.

Virginia Health Bulletin, No 2: Source text is the Virginia Health Bulletin, Vol. XVL, March 1924, Extra No. 2 which announced the Racial Integrity Act of 1924 (Senate Bill 219). See Appendix B.

Do You Identify as African American?: The words *kum buba yali, kum buba tambe* come from a folk tale, *The People Could Fly* by Virginia Hamilton. In it, Toby whispers ancient words to slaves that remind them of their forgotten power of flight.

Concerning a Problem: Source text is from a letter Mildred Loving wrote to then–Attorney General Robert F. Kennedy, asking that she and her husband be allowed to return to Virginia after the passing of the Racial Integrity Act of 1924. See Appendix E. Some of the annotations are from or inspired by "What You Didn't Know About *Loving v. Virginia*," an article by Arica L. Coleman.

We Learn in Halves: Artwork is *Ankh* by Georgie Nakima. Mixed media on canvas.

Identity Gap: The title refers to the Multiracial Identity Gap as discussed by the PEW Research Center: " . . . multiracial identity is not just the sum of the races on someone's family tree. It's more complicated than that. How you were raised, how you see yourself, and how the world sees you have a profound effect in shaping multiracial identity . . . " "I DO HAVE A RIGHT" is a nod to "I Have the Right'" taken from Dr. Maria P. Root's "Bill of Rights for People of Mixed Race Heritage." See Appendix A.

Mural of This Country: This poem is a "collage" of short, ekphrastic poems inspired by Romare Bearden's art, "pasted" together such that it can be read forward or backward. The titles of Bearden's works are *Southern*

Recall, Conjur Woman, Tomorrow I May Be Far Away, Pittsburgh Memory, Battle with Cicones, Mr. Jeremiah's Sunset Guitar, Patchwork Quilt, The Conversation, and *Jazz Village.*

Untitled Image: The shape being used is the molecular structure of melanin.

I Can't Stare Directly into the Footage: Tamir Rice was 12 years old playing with a toy gun in a Cleveland, Ohio, park. Police shot him almost immediately after arriving on the scene. Four minutes passed before police administered first aid to Rice, who died the next day.

The Field White for Harvest but the Neighbors Saw Nothing: In 2014, in Bladenboro, N.C., police found the body of Lennon Lacy, a 17-year-old student and football player, hanged by a dog leash from a swing set in the middle of a trailer park occupied almost exclusively by white residents. Police ruled his death a suicide.

Southern Cross, Thirty Feet High: On June 27, 2015, Bree Newsome scaled a 30-foot pole and removed the Confederate Flag from the South Carolina state house grounds in the aftermath of a shooting in a Charleston church. In response to police officers hailing her to come down she said, in part, "In the name of Jesus this flag has to come down . . . this flag comes down today!" The flag was removed permanently on July 10, 2015.

Mushroom Cloud: All italics are quotes from Dick Gregory in a YouTube interview with Reelblack in 2015.

APPENDIX A: "BILL OF RIGHTS FOR PEOPLE OF MIXED HERITAGE" IS A PRODUCT OF THE WORK AND TEACHING OF DR. MARIA P. ROOT, PH.D.

Bill of Rights

for

People of Mixed Heritage

I   **HAVE THE RIGHT . . .**

Not to justify my existence in this world.

Not to keep the races separate within me.

Not to justify my ethnic legitimacy.

Not to be responsible for people's discomfort with my physical or ethnic ambiguity.

I   **HAVE THE RIGHT . . .**

To identify myself differently than strangers expect me to identify.

To identify myself differently than how my parents identify me.

To identify myself differently than my brothers and sisters.

To identify myself differently in different situations.

I   **HAVE THE RIGHT . . .**

To create a vocabulary to communicate about being multiracial or multiethnic.

To change my identity over my lifetime—and more than once.

To have loyalties and identification with more than one group of people.

To freely choose whom I befriend and love.

VIRGINIA

HEALTH   BULLETIN

Vol. XVI.   MARCH. 1924.   Extra No. 2.

The New Virginia Law

To Preserve Racial Integrity

W. A. Plecker, M. I)., *Stale Registrar of Vital Statistics, Richmond, Va.*

Senate Bill 219, To preserve racial integrity, passed the House March 8, 1924, and is now a law of the State.

This bill aims at correcting a condition which only the more thought ful people of Virginia know the existence of.

It is estimated that there arc in the State from 10,000 to 20,000, possibly more, near white people, who are known to j>ossess an inter mixture of colored blood, in some cases to a slight extent it is true, but still enough to prevent them from being white.

In the past it has been i>ossible for these jicoplc to declare them selves as white, or even to have the Court so declare them. Then they have demanded the admittance of their children into the white schools, and in not a few cases have intermarried with white people.

In many counties they exist as distinct colonies holding themselves aloof from negroes, but not being admitted by the white people as of their race.

In any large gathering or school of colored |>cople, esjjccially in the cities, many will be observed who are scarcely distinguishable as colored.

These persons, however, are not white in reality, nor by the new definition of this law, that a white person is one with no trace of the blood of another race, except that a person with one-sixteenth of the American Indian, if there is no other nice mixture, may be classed as white.

Their children are likely to revert to the distinctly negro type even when all apparent evidence of mixture has disappeared.

The Virginia Bureau of Vital Statistics has Þcen called upon within one month for evidence by two lawyers employed to assist people of this type to force their children into the white public schools, and by another employed by the school trustees of a district to prevent this action.

Entered as second class matter July 28, 1908, at the Postoffice at Richmond, Va., under the Act of July 16, 1894.

APPENDIX C: SB 219, THE RACIAL INTEGRITY ACT

Virginia General Assembly
SB 219, The Racial Integrity Act, March 20, 1924

1. Be it enacted by the General Assembly of Virginia, That the State Registrar of Vital Statistics may as soon as practicable after the taking effect of this act, prepare a form whereon the racial composition of any individual, as Caucasian, negro, Mongolian, American Indian, Asiatic Indian, Malay, or any mixture thereof, or any other non-Caucasic strains, and if there be any mixture, then the racial composition of the parents and other ancestors, in so far as ascertainable, so as to show in what generation such mixture occurred, may be certified by such individual, which form shall be known as a registration certificate. The State Registrar may supply to each local registrar a sufficient number of such forms for the purpose of this act; each local registrar may personally or by deputy, as soon as possible after receiving said forms, have made thereon in duplicate a certificate of the racial composition as aforesaid, of each person resident in his district, who so desires, born before June fourteenth, nineteen hundred and twelve, which certificate shall be made over the signature of said person, or in the case of children under fourteen years of age, over the signature of a parent, guardian, or other person standing in loco parentis. One of said certificates for each person thus registering in every district shall be forwarded to the State Registrar for his files; the other shall be kept on file by the local registrar.

Every local registrar may, as soon as practicable, have such registration certificate made by or for each person in his district who so desires, born before June fourteen, nineteen hundred and twelve, for whom he has not on file a registration certificate, or a birth certificate.

2. It shall be a felony for any person wilfully or knowingly to make a registration certificate false as to color or race. The wilful making of a false registration or birth certificate shall be punished by confinement in the penitentiary for one year.

3. For each registration certificate properly made and returned to the State Registrar, the local registrar returning the same shall be entitled to a fee of twenty-five cents, to be paid by the registrant. Application for registration and for transcript may be made direct to the State Registrar, who may retain the fee for expenses of his office.

4. No marriage license shall be granted until the clerk or deputy clerk has reasonable assurance that the statements as to color of both man and woman are correct.

If there is reasonable cause to disbelieve that applicants are of pure white race, when that fact is stated, the clerk or deputy clerk shall withhold the granting of the license until satisfactory proof is produced that both applicants are "white persons" as provided for in this act.

The clerk or deputy clerk shall use the same care to assure himself that both applicants are colored, when that fact is claimed.

5. It shall hereafter be unlawful for any white person in this State to marry any save a white person, or a person with no other admixture of blood than white and American Indian. For the purpose of this act, the term "white person" shall apply only to the person who has no trace whatsoever of any blood other than Caucasian; but persons who have one-sixteenth or less of the blood of the American Indian and have no other non-Caucasic blood shall be deemed to be white persons. All laws heretofore passed and now in effect regarding the intermarriage of white and colored persons shall apply to marriages prohibited by this act.

6. For carrying out the purposes of this act and to provide the necessary clerical assistance, postage and other expenses of the State Registrar of Vital Statistics, twenty per cent of the fees received by local registrars under this act shall be paid to the State Bureau of Vital Statistics, which may be expended by the said bureau for the purposes of this act.

7. All acts or parts of acts inconsistent with this act are, to the extent of such inconsistency, hereby repealed.

APPENDIX D: 1963 ARTICLE RELATING TO MISCEGENATION LAWS, TRANSCRIBED FROM ROCKY MOUNT, NORTH CAROLINA, *TELEGRAM*, SUNDAY, NOVEMBER 10, 1963

The Rocky Mount, N. C. Telegram, Sun., Nov. 10, 1963—7A

NC Prohibits Any Marriage Between Races

BY ROBERT E. LEE
For The N. C. Bar Association

Have recent "civil rights" decisions of the U. S. Supreme Court rendered valid marriages in North Carolina between Negro and white persons?

No. The constitutionality of state statutes prohibiting the intermarriage of persons of designated races has never been ruled upon by the Supreme Court of the United States. It has declined to review several cases in which such statutes have been upheld by state courts.

The question has arisen on numerous occasions in the state and lower federal courts, and in every case, except one decided in a 4 to 3 decision by the Supreme Court of California in 1948, these state laws have been held valid.

The theory on which the constitutionality of these state statutes have been sustained is they constitute a prohibition against both races alike and confer no special privileges on either. The Supreme Court of North Carolina so held as early as 1869, at a time when the state was occupied by federal troops.

One would not be realistic, however, to conclude the present great weight of authority in favor of the constitutionality of these anti-miscegenation statutes will remain static in the light of the U. S. Supreme Court's recently growing tendency to move forward whenever racial issues are involved.

Other States Rule

To what extent are interracial marriages prohibited in the United States?

At the present time there are 21 states having statutes prohibiting certain interracial marriages. The outlawing of intermarriage of whites and Negroes is the most common. All southern states have such statutes.

Six states, including North Carolina, have regarded the matter of such importance they have by constitutional provisions prohibited their legislatures from passing any law legalizing marriages between Negroes and white persons. The present Constitution of North Carolina says such marriages "are forever prohibited."

Who Is Negro?

What constitutes a person a Negro within the meaning of the North Carolina statute?

The Supreme Court of North Carolina has said that a Negro, within the meaning of the statute which prohibits marriages "between a white person and a person of Negro descent to the third generation, inclusive," is one who has one-eighth Negro ancestry.

Thus if the person to whom ancestry in the prohibited degree is sought to be proved has only one Negro ancestor, and that a great-grandparent, it must be proved that such ancestor was of absolutely pure Negro blood. This might be extraordinarily difficult.

What Are Consequences?

What are the legal consequences of marriage performed in North Carolina between a Negro and a white person?

The purported marriage is absolutely null and void. Being a nullity, it is good for no legal purpose.

The children of a prohibited interracial marriage are illegitimate.

It is a criminal offense in North Carolina for a person with the prohibited degree of Negro ancestry to marry a white person. It is also a criminal offense for a register of deeds to issue to the parties a license or for a minister or justice of the peace to marry them, if he knows they are within the prohibited degree. The marriage is utterly null and void, and if they cohabit they may be indicted on a criminal charge of fornication.

This Is The Law

107

1151 Neal St.
N.E. Wash. D.C.
June 20, 1963

Dear sir:

I am writing to you concerning a problem we have.

5 yrs. ago my husband and I were married here in the District. We then returned to Va. to live. My husband is White, I am part negro & part indian.

At the time we did not know there was a law in Va. against mixed marriages.

Therefore we were jailed and tried in a little town of Bowling Green.

We were to leave the state to make our home.

The problem is we are not allowed to visit our families. The judge said if we enter the state within the next 30 yrs. that we will have to spend 1 yr. in jail.

We know we can't live there, but we would like to go back once and awhile to visit our families & friends.

We have 3 children and cannot afford an attorney.

We wrote to the Attorney General, he suggested that we get in touch with you

for advice.

Please help us if you can. Hope to hear from you real soon.

Yours truely,
Mr. & Mrs. Richard Loving

APPENDIX F: EXCERPT FROM ANTI-MISCEGENATION LAWS, STATE BY STATE ON THE TENNESSEE GOVERNMENT WEBSITE.

TERMS FORMERLY USED TO REPRESENT DEGREES OF BLACKNESS:

mulatto: A person of mixed race who is half white and half black. Based on the Spanish word *mulo,* meaning "mule," and implying that the person is sterile like a mule. (Another familiar misconception concerned the concept of "hybrid vigor," the idea that breeding across difference, as with dogs, creates a stronger and more attractive breed.) In some ways, this is the most shocking of all the words on these pages describing the varieties of black people with mixed blood.

quadroon or quarteron: A person with one white parent and one mulatto parent. Such a person would be 3/4 white and 1/4 black.

octoroon or metif: A person who has one white parent and one quadroon parent. Such a person would be 7/8 white and 1/8 black.

meamelouc or mamelouque: See sextaroon.

sextaroon: Also called a meamelouc or mamelouque. A person who is 1/16 black. The parents would be a full-blooded white and an octoroon.

demi-meamelouc: A person who is 1/32 black. The parents would be a full-blooded white and a sextaroon.

sangmelee: A person who is 1/64 black. The parents would be a full-blooded white and a demi-meamelouc.

griffe: A person whose parents are a full-blooded black and a mulatto. Such a person would be 3/4 black and 1/4 white. The term is also used to describe the offspring of a mulatto and an American Indian, or any person of mixed Negro and American Indian blood.

marabou: A person who is 5/8 black. The parents would be a full-blooded black and a quadroon.

sacatra: A person who is 7/8 black. The parents would be a full-blooded black and a griffe.

ACKNOWLEDGEMENTS

This book would simply not exist without the support of my family, friends, & peers, too many to name, though I will try here, begging patience & forgiveness from those I've missed. To my mom, Judy, my brother, Tyrone, and my kids, Andrea, Naticia, Mike: this manuscript and its experiences are partly mine and partly yours. I love you all.

Thanks to Callaloo, especially the generosity of Vievee Francis and Gregory Pardlo who each made me look at poetry differently (shout out to *Where's the Volta?*). Thanks to Tin House Winter Workshop and Erica Dawson for insightful instruction. Thanks also to the Breadloaf Writers Conference and all the writers I found and bonded with there. Many thanks as well to The Frost Place. I cannot overstate the impact of The Watering Hole on my writing and life. Thanks to Candace Wiley and Monifa Lemons for its existence and the tireless work needed to make it so.

Much appreciation to Angelo Geter, Lucie Berjoan, Kirwyn Sutherland, and Chavonn Shen whose feedback and critique made these poems immeasurably better than their initial drafts, and to Shane Manier whose artistic capabilities allowed some of these poems to live on paper the way I saw them in my head. Thank you a million times!

Thank you to cohorts and tribe for inspiration, for the push that only brilliance can give, and for necessary tough love: Crystal Valentine, Dave Harris, Nicholas Nichols, Nicole Homer, Marvin Hodges, Kassidi Jones, Portia Bartley, Noor Ibn Najam, Daniella Toosie-Watson, Siaara Freeman, Michael Frazier, Arriel Vinson, Jody Chan, Lucy Burns, Shakthi Shrima, Chavonn Shen.

Thanks to Ross White for endless encouragement. Thanks to Noah Stetzer, Gabrielle Calvocoressi, Tyler Mills, and Tyehimba Jess for specific generosities. Thanks to the keen, steady eye of Michael Mlekoday.

Thanks to Charisse for allowing me the time and space and support during a pandemic summer to really hammer, malleableize, and form these poems.

Thanks to the spoken word & slam communities for inspiring me, for holding me accountable, for instilling within me the desire to push boundaries. I couldn't possibly name all of the poets who've influenced me or helped me in such a small space, but know that I carry your work with me always. Thanks especially to SlamCharlotte and each team I was fortunate enough to have been part of (P.S. shout out to Southern Fried!).

And thanks, of course, to the team at Button for showing the world the power and grace of poetry, for believing in me, and for believing specifically in this work.

Many thanks to the publications who first published the following poems, or versions of them, I am forever grateful.

The Amistad	Jerry Jones Addresses His [Players] Regarding the NFL Boycott
Columbia Journal	Kodak 4200 Slide Projector Asks if I Ever Held Hands with My Father
Crabfat Magazine	The Makers
Cutthroat	Southern Cross, Thirty Feet High
Diagram	Concerning a Problem
Diode Poetry Journal	forever, a protest is just a run
	Google Image Search: Boston Massacre
Four Way Review	The Boy Is
	Homecoming, Rich Square, NC
	Inheritance
INCH #42 Sing Me A Lesser Wound	I Can't Stare Directly into the Footage
	Etymology of 'Boy'
	The Field White for Harvest but the Neighbors Saw Nothing
	Like Prophets of Baal
	I Love the Hometown I Had to Leave
Juked	Ode to Black-*ish*
The Lichening	The Plantation Bears Witness
	Spiritual Rising from a Cotton Field Burning
Litmosphere	Imagine Me
Poetry Online	Language of Composition
Roanoke Review	Blessings
	Virginia Health Bulletin, Extra No. 2

ABOUT THE AUTHOR

Junious "Jay" Ward is a poet living in Charlotte, NC, and the author of *Sing Me a Lesser Wound* (Bull City Press). Jay is a National Poetry Slam champion and Individual World Poetry Slam champion who has toured nationally. He has attended and/or received support from Breadloaf Writers Conference, Callaloo, The Frost Place, Tin House Winter Workshop, and The Watering Hole, and currently serves as a Program Director for BreatheInk and Vice-Chair for The Watering Hole. His poems can be found in *Four Way Review*, *DIAGRAM*, *Columbia Journal*, *The Amistad*, *Diode Poetry Journal*, and elsewhere.

OTHER BOOKS BY BUTTON POETRY

If you enjoyed this book, please consider checking out some of our others, below. Readers like you allow us to keep broadcasting and publishing. Thank you!

Desireé Dallagiacomo, *SINK*

Dave Harris, *Patricide*

Michael Lee, *The Only Worlds We Know*

Raych Jackson, *Even the Saints Audition*

Brenna Twohy, *Swallowtail*

Porsha Olayiwola, *i shimmer sometimes, too*

Jared Singer, *Forgive Yourself These Tiny Acts of Self-Destruction*

Adam Falkner, *The Willies*

George Abraham, *Birthright*

Omar Holmon, *We Were All Someone Else Yesterday*

Rachel Wiley, *Fat Girl Finishing School*

Bianca Phipps, *crown noble*

Natasha T. Miller, *Butcher*

Kevin Kantor, *Please Come Off-Book*

Ollie Schminkey, *Dead Dad Jokes*

Reagan Myers, *Afterwards*

L.E. Bowman, *What I Learned From the Trees*

Patrick Roche, *A Socially Acceptable Breakdown*

Rachel Wiley, *Revenge Body*

Ebony Stewart, *BloodFresh*

Ebony Stewart, *Home.Girl.Hood.*

Kyle Tran Mhyre, *Not A Lot of Reasons to Sing, but Enough*

Steven Willis, *A Peculiar People*

Topaz Winters, *So, Stranger*

Darius Simpson, *Never Catch Me*

Blythe Baird, *Sweet, Young, & Worried*

Siaara Freeman, *Urbanshee*

Robert Wood Lynn, *How to Maintain Eye Contact*

Available at buttonpoetry.com/shop and more!

FORTHCOMING BOOKS BY BUTTON POETRY

Usman Hameedi, *Staying Right Here*
Sierra DeMulder, *Ephemera*
Matt Mason, *Rock Stars*
Anita D., *Sitcom Material*
Miya Coleman, *Cotton Mouth*

BUTTON POETRY BEST SELLERS

Neil Hilborn, *Our Numbered Days*
Hanif Abdurraqib, *The Crown Ain't Worth Much*
Sabrina Benaim, *Depression & Other Magic Tricks*
Rudy Francisco, *Helium*
Rachel Wiley, *Nothing Is Okay*
Neil Hilborn, *The Future*
Phil Kaye, *Date & Time*
Andrea Gibson, *Lord of the Butterflies*
Blythe Baird, *If My Body Could Speak*
Andrea Gibson, *You Better Be Lightning*

Available at buttonpoetry.com/shop and more!